A PERSONAL PORTRAIT
OF
The Royal Family

COLIN EDWARDS

CANDY JAR BOOKS

A Personal Portrait of the Royal Family

FIRST EDITION
- 2014 -

Photographs and text © Colin Edwards 2014
Edited by Hayley Cox

Published by
Candy Jar Books, 113-116 Bute Street, Cardiff, CF10 5EQ
www.candy-jar.co.uk

A catalogue record of this book is available from the British Library

ISBN: 978-0-9571548-4-1

Printed and bound in the UK by
Cambrian Printers, Aberystwyth, SY23 3TN

*This book is dedicated to my beloved parents: the late
Nora and Rob Edwards.*

FOREWORD

During my time as HM Lord Lieutenant for Clwyd, I became aware of Mr Edwards' lifelong interest and support for The Queen and the rest of the Royal Family.

This book is a record of that interest and the work of the Royal Family. It is illustrated by the other passion of Mr Edwards, photography.

The pictures are a fascinating illustration of an important period in British history.

Trefor G. Jones ESQ. CBE, CVO
St Asaph, Denbighshire

Gloucester Cathedral, April 2003

INTRODUCTION

This book is a pictorial record of my many encounters with three of the most popular royal ladies of the twentieth century. It charts my meetings with Her Majesty The Queen, the late Queen Mother and the late Diana, Princess of Wales, as well as other members of the Royal Family during the last thirty years.

I have often been asked why and when I became fascinated by the Royal Family. My interest began with the Coronation. Elizabeth II was just twenty-seven years old when she was crowned Queen in Westminster Abbey on 2nd June 1953. I was then a twelve-year-old schoolboy and watched the celebrations on our new television set with my parents, sister, many friends, relations and neighbours. I was mesmerized by the procession, ceremony and the pageantry. Sixty years later, I am still an ardent Royalist.

I have had the honour and privilege of photographing members of the Royal Family on many occasions throughout the United Kingdom. It has been a memorable and exciting experience, and the photographs in this book are my personal tribute to our beloved Queen, who has served our nation and the Commonwealth with devotion and dedication for over sixty years.

Long may she reign over us!

Colin Edwards
Ruthin, North Wales, February 2014

CHAPTER 1
Her Majesty The Queen

Manchester, February 2008

I first met Her Majesty The Queen in May 1982 in Manchester, although I had seen her many times from the 1950s onwards, including at the State Funeral of Sir Winston Churchill in January 1965, and her Silver Jubilee celebrations in 1977.

I have always been interested in photography and in the early 1980s started going to The Queen's walkabouts with my camera. Since then my Royal visits have taken me to many towns and cities across Britain. On my travels I go by train and often stay in hotels.

Royalists like me have to arrive at least two hours early to get a good position behind the barrier. We can then speak to the Royals, hand over flowers or gifts, and take our photographs.

Attendance at a Royal visit involves stamina and patience but can bring great happiness and satisfaction.

It has been a great honour and privilege meeting our much-loved Queen so many times. These memories will stay with me for the rest of my life.

Aberystwyth, May 1996

Burnley, November 1987

The Queen is used to seeing me at the events she attends. On this occasion she spent time talking to me outside the town hall in Burnley. I asked her if I could take another photograph as I knew I would not see her for some time. She responded, much to my amusement, 'I'm not sure about that, you turn up everywhere!'

People in their seventies, like myself, clearly remember the Coronation. I was twelve years old and in my first year at grammar school. Excitement had been mounting since Her Majesty had become Queen following the death of her father, King George VI on 6th February 1952.

A few weeks before the great day, my sister and I arrived home from school to find a television (black and white only of course) in the corner of the living room – Mum and Dad had kept it a secret and surprised us!

We were the second family in our street to own a television. Mum invited a group of friends, relatives and neighbours to watch the Coronation on our set. Our living room was rather overcrowded! Television coverage lasted for about five hours, and so Mum was kept busy making sandwiches and serving endless cups of tea.

At the conclusion of the ceremony, my sister and I joined many other children at the church hall for a party with plenty of food and games. It was supposed to be a street party, but the rain hindered our plans.

A few days later, a fancy dress parade was held for children and adults as part of the continued celebrations. I won a prize for my costume; I had a cardboard box on my head to represent a television set and cards with job descriptions all over my clothes. I was dressed as *What's My Line?* one of the most popular shows on television at the time.

Soon after the Coronation the Mayor of Ruthin visited all the schools and presented a commemorative mug to each pupil. This mug was the first item in my now vast collection of royal commemorative china.

Another highlight of our Coronation celebrations was the colour screening of *A Queen is Crowned* at our local cinema, which was packed with children from all the nearby schools.

It was just a few weeks later, July 1953, that I first saw The Queen, when she and The Duke of Edinburgh visited the National Eisteddfod, near Rhyl, during her tour of Wales. I was with my mother, sister and other relations, and we were so excited seeing our beautiful young Queen arriving in her open car.

To the right is the first photograph I ever took of HM The Queen. I used a cheap, disposable camera at the Silver Jubilee celebrations.

The Queen was celebrating twenty-five years on the throne. Many events were organised, including a Service of Thanksgiving held at Saint Paul's Cathedral and attended by Her Majesty, the entire Royal Family and Heads of State from all over the world.

I travelled to London overnight by coach, arriving early in the morning to secure a place in the front row. I had a close-up view of the Royals in their carriages, particularly of The Queen and Prince Philip in the magnificent Gold State Coach, last used for the Coronation.

After the service The Queen and the Royal Family were invited to lunch with the Lord Mayor of London at Guildhall. Later, they returned to Buckingham Palace in open carriages. As Her Majesty's carriage drew level with me, I spontaneously called out, 'God bless you Ma'am, we love you!' She looked quite moved and gave me a warm smile in acknowledgement.

Two days later, I saw the spectacular firework display from Westminster Bridge. Since then I have attended the London Jubilee celebrations in 2002 and 2012, and I hope to celebrate Her Majesty's Platinum Jubilee (seventy years on the throne) in 2022!

HM The Queen and The Duke of Edinburgh

HRH Princess Margaret and Lord Mountbatten of Burma

The Queen's Birthday Parade, June 1961

I attended The Queen's annual Birthday Parade for the second time in June 1961. At that time I didn't have a camera of my own so used my mother's thirty-year-old box camera. Despite its age I'm really pleased with the photographs I was able to capture as Her Majesty took the salute outside Buckingham Palace. For many years the public were allowed to stand in front of the Victoria Memorial, but for security reasons this is no longer possible.

In the photograph above The Duke of Edinburgh is on The Queen's left and on her right is her uncle the late Duke of Gloucester. In the distance you can just about make out the late Queen Mother, Princess Anne and the late Princess Royal on the balcony.

Above: London, July 1988

Below: London, June 2006

14

G arter Day 1986 was the first time I saw this colourful procession. The Royal Family made their way to Saint George's Chapel, at Windsor Castle, for the annual order of the Garter service.

It's always a thrill to see so many members of the Royal Family walking in procession and later returning to the castle in magnificent carriages.

The service is always held on the Monday following Trooping the Colour and before the first day of Royal Ascot.

In 2013 the Garter procession was as impressive as ever. In the absence of HRH The Duke of Edinburgh, who had just been discharged from hospital following an exploratory operation, we wondered who would accompany HM The Queen in procession. I was delighted to see that Her Majesty was accompanied by her two heirs TRH The Prince of Wales and the Duke of Cambridge.

Trooping the Colour – The Queen's Birthday Parade

This colourful annual event on Horse Guard's Parade is always held on the second or third Saturday in June, even though Her Majesty's official birthday is the 21st April. From 1953 to 1958 I watched the ceremony on television, but in 1959 I was able to travel to London and experience the ceremony first-hand. I'll never forget the pageantry, colour, military bands and, of course, seeing The Queen in her scarlet tunic and dark blue skirt riding side-saddle (for the last time) on her horse, Burmese.

For over fifty years I have attended as many Birthday Parades as I could. I remember in 1961 The Queen appeared on the balcony for the RAF flypast, holding sixteen-month-old Prince Andrew in her arms, much to the delight of the crowd. In 1969 that icon of the air Concorde flew over the palace, saluting Her Majesty. The cheers were deafening.

The 1981 Birthday Parade was memorable for two reasons: Lady Diana Spencer attended for the first time, and it was also the year a deranged youth shot blanks at The Queen just before she arrived at Horse Guards Parade. Had the bullets been real, he could so easily have killed Her Majesty. She expertly controlled her horse and bravely continued on.

Diana attended the ceremony for the last time in 1992 before her separation from Prince Charles in the December of that year.

The 2001 Parade proved to be the last one The Queen Mother would attend. She had been present at the Birthday Parades of four monarchs from 1923 to 2001: King George V (her father-in-law), King Edward VIII (her brother-in-law), King George VI (her husband) and her daughter Queen Elizabeth II.

In 2011 a new member of the Royal Family joined the celebrations – Kate, HRH The Duchess of Cambridge. She shared a carriage with the Duchess of Cornwall and Prince Harry. Her husband, William, rode behind his grandmother for the first time, wearing his uniform as Colonel of the Irish Guards.

People from all over the world come to London for the pomp and pageantry that Trooping the Colour promises. It's an event that always make me feel patriotic and proud to be British.

Trooping the Colour, London, June 1986

The Queen has ridden a succession of different horses since her first appearance at Trooping the Colour in 1947. June 1986 was the last time Her Majesty rode side-saddle to her Birthday Parade. Burmese, the horse she had ridden since 1969, was given to Her Majesty by the Royal Canadian Mounted Police in the same year.

Since 1987 she has been driven to Horse Guards Parade in Queen Victoria's small ivory phaeton carriage, and since 2003 Prince Philip has accompanied her.

Trooping the Colour, London, June 2005

WINDSOR CASTLE

21st April, 1992.

Dear Mr Edwards.

No Royal visit would be complete without a
selection of splendid Edwards photographs, and
The Queen was delighted to see you in Chester
and to receive those lovely photographs of
Wakefield. Her Majesty thanks you for your
kind Easter and birthday cards, and sends you
her best wishes.

Yours sincerely,

Kenneth Scott.

(KENNETH SCOTT)

R. Colin Edwards., Esq.

Chelmsford, July 1988

Manchester, April 2007

Above: Trooping the Colour, London, June 1989

Below: Welshpool, 21st April 1989 (Her Majesty's 63rd birthday)

WINDSOR CASTLE

24th April, 1989.

Dear Mr Edwards,

The Queen was very pleased to see a
familiar face in the crowd at Welshpool on
Friday, and to receive from you your handsome
card of birthday greetings and the lovely
photographs which you took during Her
Majesty's visit to Birmingham on Maundy
Thursday. The Queen now has a splendid
collection of your photographs, which she
keeps as a memento of her various visits at
which you have been present. She sends you
her warm thanks and best wishes.

Yours sincerely,

Kenneth Scott

(KENNETH SCOTT)

R. C. Edwards, Esq.

Her Majesty's visit to the Royal Show in July 1989 was an informal and relaxed one. As usual, I presented her with a framed photograph. After she accepted it she turned to a lady standing next to me and said, 'He is a very good photographer, you know.' It was so lovely to hear such praise.

Crewe, July 1987

I took these photographs in 1989 and gave The Queen a copy of them in Worcester four months later. In 2002 I won a national newspaper's competition with the photograph below.

Carlisle, May 1991

Edinburgh, July 1997

Lincoln, April 2000

Windsor, 21st April 2006 (Her Majesty's 80th birthday)

17th June, 1988.

Dear Mr Edwards

    I am commanded by The Queen to thank you for your letter of 14th June. Her Majesty was glad that you had enjoyed the recent Beating Retreat and the Birthday Parade on Horse Guards.

    Her Majesty notes that you will be going to St. Christopher's Hospice in Sydenham in August and I feel sure that she will need no reminder about the identity of the man in the Union Jack hat.

James Oulee
Henlein

R. Colin Edwards, Esq.

Above: Carlisle, May 1991

Opposite: Derby, May 1992

Below: Chester, April 1992

I often enter Royal photography competitions and won a competition in
1992 with this photograph.

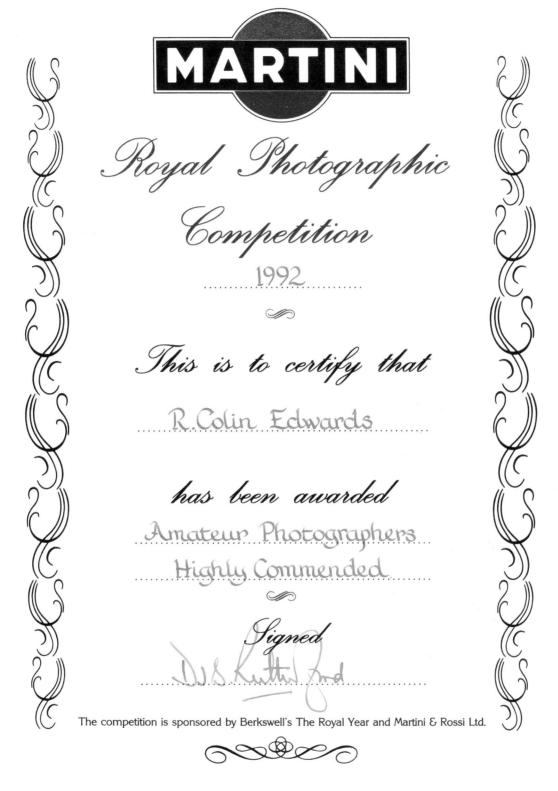

MARTINI

Royal Photographic

Competition

1992

This is to certify that

R. Colin Edwards

has been awarded

Amateur Photographers

Highly Commended

Signed

The competition is sponsored by Berkswell's The Royal Year and Martini & Rossi Ltd.

Manchester, December 1996

On this walkabout (photograph above) The Queen congratulated me on the commendation I had received for a photograph of her.

Northampton, October 1992

Sandringham, August 2000

In the photograph above The Queen is holding a jigsaw that was given to her by my friend.

West Newton, Norfolk, February 1996

Above: Nottingham, March 1997

Below: Westminster Abbey, London, 20th November 1997 (The Queen and Prince Philip's Golden Wedding Anniversary)

This photograph was taken in London in 1996 as The Queen and President Mandela of South Africa, who was on a State Visit, were leaving Horse Guards Parade in a carriage procession. Later that day, I met him at Westminster Abbey, and I welcomed him to Great Britain. He replied, 'Thank you, you are so kind. I am so pleased to be here.'

Later, I sent him a copy of this photograph and was delighted to receive a letter of thanks from his private secretary, together with a signed photograph of the great man.

I will never forget meeting him.

BALMORAL CASTLE

26th August, 1989.

Dear Mr Edwards,

 The Queen has commanded me to thank you
for your letter of 24th August. It was, as
always, a pleasure for Her Majesty to hear
from you, and she was most grateful for the
kind thoughts which you expressed in your
letter. The Queen sends you her best
wishes.

Yours sincerely,

Kenneth Scott.

(KENNETH SCOTT)

R. C. Edwards, Esq.

Wolverhampton, July 1994

Bristol, June 1995

My friends and I saw Her Majesty arrive (photograph above) at a Police Headquarters in Bristol. As she passed, she smiled and waved at the crowds but could not stop and greet us as she was due to open the building.

As we were about to leave, one of her bodyguards approached me, 'Colin, The Queen has asked me to tell you that when she leaves the car will stop and she will accept your flowers and gifts.' We waited for an hour, and, sure enough, the car stopped, and The Queen reached through the window for our flowers and my photograph.

I thanked her for her kindness and took this photo. She thanked us for waiting. She could have easily just driven passed us. It was lovely to hear that Her Majesty appreciates our loyalty and support.

Above: Bolsover, July 1997

Below: Norfolk, February 2000

HM The Queen launched the Royal Yacht Britannia on 16th April 1953 at Clydeside. During the next forty-four years the yacht took Her Majesty and members of the Royal Family on official and private visits all over the world.

I had the pleasure of seeing Britannia on five occasions between 1993 and 1997 (in Liverpool, Portsmouth, Oban, Scrabster and on the Thames in London).

In 1994 the government decided that the yacht had reached the end of its life and that it would be decommissioned. In December 1997 at the ceremony in Portsmouth, The Queen was visibly moved as she said farewell to her beloved floating home.

I travelled to Caithness, in the north of Scotland, to see the Royal Family and take the photograph on the opposite page. I took it as The Queen and Queen Mother were getting ready to drive to the Castle of Mey, where they enjoyed lunch and tea before continuing to Aberdeen. It is the only time I have seen Her Majesty wearing a headscarf.

This was the Royal Family's final cruise on the yacht before it was decommissioned. It was the end of an era. I remember Her Majesty graciously remarking to me, 'Nothing lasts forever.' Two years later, in July 1999, I visited Britannia in its new permanent home at Leith, near Edinburgh. I found it a fascinating and quite emotional experience.

Above: Manchester, March 2012

Opposite: Chester, April 1992

Below: Edinburgh, July 1997

Above: Norwich, April 1996

Below: Lincoln, April 2000

E II R

The Lord Chamberlain is commanded by Her Majesty to invite

Mr Colin Edwards

to a Garden Party
at Buckingham Palace
on Tuesday 22nd July 1997 from 4 to 6 pm

This card does not admit

In the Spring of 1997 I received a letter from the Lord Lieutenant of Cheshire, informing me that a member of the public in Macclesfield, where I was then living, had nominated me for an invitation to the Royal Garden Party! It was quite unexpected, and I was so grateful to the person who nominated me.

The Garden Party fell on a lovely sunny day. I had an excellent view of Her Majesty as she and the other members of the Royal Family arrived. She spotted me as she walked amongst the guests and offered a casual greeting. As it was a formal occasion, I bowed and said, 'Good afternoon, Your Majesty.' Cameras are not allowed at Garden Parties, and it seemed strange not taking a photograph of her.

I thoroughly enjoyed the delicious food and listening to the military bands. I saw The Queen later in the day, and she asked me if I had enjoyed it. I said, 'Very much so. Thank you, Ma'am, it has been an unforgettable day.'

Above: Bradford, March 1997

Opposite: Birmingham, October 1998

Below: Rochdale, November 1994

In the photograph below Her Majesty's wrist is in plaster. She had been injured in a riding accident and was using her silk scarf as a sling.

Windsor, 21st April 2006 (The Queen's 80th birthday)

Sandringham, 25th December 1996

West Newton, Norfolk, February 1994

Sandringham, 4th August 1996 (The Queen Mother's 96th birthday)

On a very wet day in October 2000, Her Majesty opened the new Lowry Centre in Salford, near Manchester. I was quite sure that her walkabout would be cancelled, but she did not disappoint. She came out to see us, holding her see-through umbrella.

The Queen's first words to me were, 'You haven't had far to come today.' She had remembered where I lived!

Above: Bolsover, July 1997

Below: Cambridge, October 1993

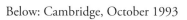

Right: Birmingham, October 1993

Below left: Coventry, March 2000

Below right: Runcorn, July 1998

The day after The Queen opened the Bridgewater Hall, Manchester, she was in the city centre again to see the damage caused by the IRA bomb six months earlier. I showed her a picture of myself with The Queen Mother, taken in London, which was in *The Times* the previous week. She said she had seen it, adding, 'You are often in the papers.'

Above: Walsall, May 2000

Below: Huddersfield, May 2007

On 6th February 2002 The Queen celebrated fifty years on the throne – the first monarch to do so since Queen Victoria celebrated her Golden Jubilee in 1887.

It had been announced that the celebrations would take place in early June and consist of two concerts in the Buckingham Palace garden, a National Service of Thanksgiving at Saint Paul's Cathedral (followed by a parade down The Mall) and an appearance on the balcony.

My friends and I arrived in London on 3rd June and found a vacant space at the bottom of The Mall. Later that evening, by kind permission of Her Majesty, we enjoyed a champagne picnic in the Palace garden. This picnic preceded the pop concert (I had entered the ballot and successfully secured tickets). The entire Royal Family was in attendance, and I particularly enjoyed the performances by Dame Shirley Bassey, Sir Cliff Richard and Sir Paul McCartney – all favourites of mine. The concert ended with a magnificent firework display – it was an unforgettable evening.

It was a cold night and sleeping was almost impossible on the pavement! By 7am sleeping bags had been rolled up and tents dismantled, but it would be some time before we left The Mall.

Time soon passed, and the carriage procession from the Palace to Saint Paul's began. Finally, the moment we had all been waiting for – the Gold State Coach came into sight, taking The Queen and Prince Philip to the Service of Thanksgiving.

We were opposite the choir that had entertained us all morning, and as the State Coach passed they performed *Zadok the Priest*, which was also sung at the Coronation. It sent a tingle down my spine, and I felt so proud to be British.

Before returning to the palace the Royal Family walked on each side of The Mall, chatting to members of the public. Prince William, The Princess Royal and The Earl and Countess of Wessex walked down our side. The walkabout had not been announced, so it was an unexpected bonus.

Soon after, The Queen and Prince Philip drove down The Mall in an open Range Rover and joined their family on a podium to watch the parade. This mainly consisted of colourfully dressed dancers from the famous Notting Hill Carnival. The atmosphere was electric.

The Royal Family arrived back at the palace as the police brought thousands of people down The Mall for the balcony appearance. The chanting of 'We want The Queen' was deafening, and when she finally appeared the crowd erupted. The Queen was joined by all her family and was visibly moved when the vast crowds sang *Rule Britannia*, *Land of Hope and Glory* and, of course, *God Save The Queen*. The flypast brought the celebrations to a close – a day I'll remember for the rest of my life.

I took this photograph after the Maundy service at Liverpool Cathedral in April 2004, on The Queen's traditional walkabout.

A man near me spoke to her with a broad Liverpool accent and said something which greatly amused Her Majesty. She is well known for her interest in the way people speak and, apparently, is an excellent mimic.

Lincoln, April 2000

I met The Queen in Bangor in June 2002 during her Golden Jubilee tour of Wales. It was the first time I had met her since the death of The Queen Mother three months earlier. Before presenting Her Majesty with my gift to commemorate her jubilee, I took the opportunity to sympathise with her. As The Queen looked at the photograph I had given her, she said, 'My mother lived to great age and had a wonderful life.'

Hereford, May 1996

Weston-Super-Mare, July 2007

Hanley, October 1999

On 21st April 2006 The Queen celebrated her eightieth birthday, the first monarch to become an octogenarian since Queen Victoria in 1899. Three Queen Consorts have also celebrated their eightieth birthdays: Queen Alexandra in 1924, Queen Mary in 1947 and, of course, Queen Elizabeth, The Queen Mother in 1980 – who also celebrated her ninetieth and 100th birthdays!

It had been announced that The Queen would celebrate her milestone birthday at Windsor Castle and would carry out a walkabout in the town centre.

My friends and I arrived at the castle early on the morning of the 21st April. A military band entertained us while we waited for Her Majesty. At 11am she appeared at the King Henry VIII gate to tumultuous cheering. Her Majesty made her way slowly along the barriers, accepting cards and flowers and chatting with her loyal subjects, who had been waiting for many hours. I presented her with a poem and a framed photograph.

Two months later, a Service of Thanksgiving was held at Saint Paul's Cathedral, followed by another walkabout. As usual, my friends and I were in the right place at the right time!

In August I enjoyed seeing a collection of hundreds of cards Her Majesty had received for her birthday, mainly cards made by children, displayed in Buckingham Palace.

HM The Queen celebrated sixty years on the throne on 6th February 2012 – the only monarch to celebrate a Diamond Jubilee since her great-great grandmother Queen Victoria celebrated hers in 1897.

It had been announced that this historic event would be celebrated in London in early June and that Her Majesty would undertake a nationwide tour to meet as many people as possible between March and July 2012.

I travelled to Norfolk to see The Queen on the actual anniversary (6th February), when she visited King's Lynn Town Hall, near Sandringham. It had snowed heavily and was bitterly cold, but our spirits were high, and we all cheered when Her Majesty left the town hall. She graciously accepted flowers and cards; I presented her with a poem to commemorate her Diamond Jubilee and told her what a great honour it had been meeting her so often.

I was fortunate enough to meet The Queen four times during the Diamond Jubilee tour, but my friend and I still travelled to London for the focal celebrations. We travelled down on 2nd June, ready for the events held over the next three days. On the evening of the 2nd, we enjoyed a wonderful concert at the Royal Albert Hall, comprising of popular patriotic music with audience participation and flag waving! The following day, we arrived early on the embankment for the River Pageant, which composed of 1000 boats from all over the country and the Commonwealth. Unfortunately, the weather couldn't have been worse – cold and wet. But it was still an unforgettable sight and an event not likely to be repeated ever again.

On Monday 4th June we arrived at St James' Park in good time to watch the next concert on big screens. This took place at the Victoria Memorial and the firework display at the end was magnificent!

The next day we arrived at Whitehall, opposite the Cenotaph, where we had an excellent view of Her Majesty and other members of the Royal Family as they travelled back to Buckingham Palace after lunch at Westminster Hall.

I returned home with happy memories of the unforgettable Diamond Jubilee celebrations.

2013 was Her Majesty's jubilee year, celebrating the sixtieth anniversary of the Coronation. Her Majesty is the second British monarch to celebrate this historic anniversary – Queen Victoria was the first in June 1898.

As part of the celebrations, The Queen was accompanied by HRH The Duke of Edinburgh and all the senior members of the Royal Family at the Service of Thanksgiving at Westminster Abbey, where Her Majesty was crowned. A few weeks later, a three day Coronation Festival was held in the grounds of Buckingham Palace, with plenty of festivities, including a concert.

The Palace was transformed to mark the occasion. Visitors were treated to an exhibition on the Coronation. The Ballroom was transformed, displaying items including: The Queen's magnificent Coronation dress and robe; The Duke of Edinburgh's uniform, robe and coronet; the dresses and robes worn by the late Queen Mother and the late Princess Margaret, as well as the outfits worn by four-year-old Prince Charles and two-year-old Princess Anne. The Prince's personal invitation was also displayed, along with jewellery worn by The Queen.

Coronation banquets had been held on 3rd and 4th June 1953, and the table in the State Dining Room had been dressed to recreate the magnificent settings.

CHAPTER 2
Her Majesty Queen Elizabeth The Queen Mother 1900-2002

I have so many happy memories of The Queen Mother between 1984 and 2001. She was a unique lady who radiated warmth and was genuinely interested in everyone she met.

Her Majesty's birthday celebrations at Clarence House were the highlight of the year for many of her admirers. Crowds of people would travel to London, even from abroad. For the last ten years of her life, it became necessary to camp out as so many people wanted to see her on her walkabouts.

From 1988 to 2001 I composed a poem for each birthday, and her Majesty graciously allowed me to read it to her. It became an annual tradition!

In January 2000 I held an exhibition of photographs of Her Majesty to celebrate her 100th birthday, at Dersingham Library, near Sandringham. She graciously accepted my invitation and attended on 25th January. She was accompanied by her lady-in-waiting and a bodyguard. I was so pleased that she could attend.

Sadly, The Queen Mother died on Easter Saturday 30th March 2002. I was on holiday in France at the time, and I immediately made arrangements to travel to London for the funeral. The day before the funeral a friend and I attended Her Majesty's lying-in-state in Westminster Hall. This was a really moving experience, and I will never forget it. It was a bitterly cold night, and we camped out with many other people outside Westminster Abbey for her funeral on 9th April.

People wept as though they had lost a close relation. It was a very emotional day, but I felt so proud and fortunate to have met our beloved Queen Mum so often during the previous seventeen years.

This is the first photograph I took of The Queen Mother. It was July 1980, and I was in the right place at the right time (which has often been the case over the years).

I was spending a few days in London and, on the day before returning home, went to Clarence House. The door was wide open, so I thought Her Majesty would either be driving out or returning home. I spoke to a friendly policeman, who informed me that The Queen Mother would be returning from an engagement shortly, so I decided to wait for her.

As she stood on the step of her car, The Queen Mum saw me and smiled and waved as I took this photograph. The door closed, and I left on cloud nine. It was a very personal and unexpected incident.

Above: London, November 1985

Below: Clarence House, London, 4th August 1987

Credit: Mark Stewart

This was my very first meeting with The Queen Mother, on her eighty-fourth birthday, 4th August 1984. She is holding my birthday gift – a book about roses, one of her favourite flowers.

HM The Queen Mother and HM The Queen at Sandringham 4th August 1991

After the Royal Family's appearance during The Queen Mother's birthday celebrations in 1992, one of the press photographers told me he had heard The Queen say, 'Look, Mummy, there's Colin!'

HM The Queen Mother and HRH Prince Charles in London, 4th August 2000
(Her Majesty's 100th birthday)

A few weeks before The Queen Mother celebrated her ninetieth birthday, my family was shaken by the death of a much-loved relation; sadly, my own beloved mother passed away. She was the woman who raised me and stimulated my lifelong interest in the Royal Family.

Within my correspondence to Her Majesty, I told her about my mother's death. Having already received a warm, sympathetic letter from her, I was touched when, on Her Majesty's birthday walkabout, she came up to me and said, 'I was so sorry to hear about your sad loss.' It was a typical gesture from a great lady who was always interested in people from all walks of life.

BUCKINGHAM PALACE

17th July, 1990

Dear Mr. Edwards,

    I am commanded by The Queen to thank you for your letter of 12th July. Her Majesty was sorry to learn of your Mother's death and sends you and your family her sincere sympathy in your sad loss.

    Yours sincerely,

(KENNETH SCOTT)

R. Colin Edwards, Esq.

Wolferton, Norfolk, August 1996

Above: West Newton, Norfolk, February 1992

Below: London, October 1997

Above: Clarence House, London, 4th August 1993

Below: London, July 2001

This photograph was taken when The Queen Mother attended a service at Wick Parish Church, Caithness, in 1994. She said, 'Are you enjoying your holiday? You're a long way from home!'

I presented a copy of this photograph to The Queen a few months later, and during the summer of 1995 a friend saw it in the Drawing Room at Sandringham! The following year, I saw it there myself.

Later, on a walkabout, I thanked Her Majesty for displaying it; she said, 'It's a very good one.'

The celebrations to mark the fiftieth anniversary of VE Day and VJ Day were held in London with vast crowds in attendance.

On the anniversary of VE Day, The Queen Mother made a short speech at Hyde Park. She and the King inspired the nation during the Second World War, and Her Majesty had famously said, 'I'm glad we've been bombed. Now I can look the East End in the face.'

The main event was the appearance on the Palace balcony of the three Royal ladies – The Queen, Queen Mother and Princess Margaret.

My abiding memory of this historic event is the concert on the forecourt of the Palace, where everybody sang old wartime songs led by Dame Vera Lynn, Sir Cliff Richard and the late Sir Harry Secombe.

In August 1995 the fiftieth anniversary of VJ Day was celebrated with a parade down The Mall. I had a superb view and was standing opposite the Royal Family. I was so pleased to see Diana with Charles and their two young sons, William and Harry.

Clarence House, London, 4th August 1992

Above: Scrabster, Caithness, August 1997

Below: Flitcham, Norfolk, January 1999

London, November 1988

HM The Queen Mother's Visit to Tain, Scotland, August 1991

I spent two weeks touring Scotland in August 1991, and, in addition to seeing HM The Queen at Balmoral and at Crathie Kirk, I drove north to see The Queen Mother in Tain. One of Her Majesty's engagements was a visit to the historic church, and I thought I would go and wait for her. She looked so surprised to see me, 'Are you on holiday, you're a long way from home!'

She then turned to the Lord Lieutenant and introduced me as 'a friend from England.'

Clarence House, London, 4th August 1990 (Her Majesty's 90th birthday)

In this photograph Her Majesty is highly amused by a small bottle of gin and tonic given to her by my friend. Apparently, this was her favourite tipple.

London, June 1997

In the spring of 1996 I was contacted by a television company commissioned by the BBC to make a film about a royal watcher – I was asked if I would like to be the subject. I thought it would be fun and interesting so agreed to take part in the programme. Filming started at Sandringham Church on The Queen Mother's ninety-sixth birthday on 4th August.

Over the next seven months I was filmed meeting The Queen, Prince Charles, Princess Diana and The Queen Mum at walkabouts. The programme was finally shown on 24th June 1997. The filming had been a fascinating experience. The cameraman also interviewed and filmed me on The Mall three months later when I camped out for Diana's funeral, for a programme on that sad and unforgettable day.

This photograph was taken the day after the documentary about my Royal visits was shown on television. The Queen Mother said to me, 'I saw your film last night!'

I asked her if she enjoyed it, and she said, 'Oh yes, very much. You cover a lot of ground don't you?'

CLARENCE HOUSE
S.W.1

9th November,
1981

Dear Mr. Edwards,

Queen Elizabeth
The Queen Mother has asked me
to write and thank you for the
three photographs which you
have sent to Her Majesty.

They really are very
good pictures and you must have
been standing in a good position
to get them.   The Queen Mother
thought it very kind of you to
send her these copies.

Yours sincerely,

Olivia Mulholland

Lady-in-Waiting

R. Colin Edwards, Esq.

Above: London, October 1997

Below: Trooping the Colour, London June 1986

Following a service at the Church of Saint Mary Magdalene in August 1999, The Queen Mother drove down the road in her buggy, accepting cards and flowers. A friend gave her a tiny birthday cake, and she laughed, saying, 'It won't take long to eat it!'

A few days later, she celebrated her ninety-ninth birthday at Clarence House.

Left: Flitcham, Norfolk, January 1999

Bottom Left: Flitcham, Norfolk, January 1999

Bottom Right: Clarence House, 4th August 1995

In November 1998 I broke my arm after slipping on an icy pavement. When I sent my usual Christmas card to The Queen Mother, I told her about the accident.

A few weeks later, I met her outside the church at Flitcham, Norfolk, not far from Sandringham. Her first words to me were, 'I hope your arm has mended now.' I thanked her for her concern, and she said, 'We were all so sorry to hear about your accident.'

London, 4th August 1993

Scrabster, Caithness, August 1997

In May 1999 The Queen Mother unveiled a memorial at St Paul's Cathedral in memory of the thousands of Londoners killed in the Blitz during the Second World War. She spoke to members of the public after the ceremony, and I was able to tell her about the losses my own family suffered. With a sad expression she said, 'I'm so sorry. Those poor people, they suffered so much.'

Above: London, June 1995

Opposite: London, April 1999

Below: London, June 1997

In November 1999 I wrote to Sir Alastair Aird, Private Secretary to The Queen Mother, inviting Her Majesty to visit my exhibition of photographs to celebrate her 100th birthday on 4th August 2000, at Dersingham Library, near Sandringham. My exhibition opened to the public on 17th January 2000, which happened to be my fifty-ninth birthday.

I received a letter from Lady Angela Oswald a few days before I left for Norfolk, confirming that Her Majesty would be delighted to visit. I will never forget that day. At 11am on 25th January the royal car arrived, and The Queen Mother stepped out wearing royal blue (one of her favourite colours), supported by her walking stick.

As I walked with her to the library entrance, I thanked her for her visit, and she said how much she had been looking forward to seeing my photographs. As I escorted Her Majesty and Lady Angela around the exhibition, The Queen Mother frequently recalled the occasions I had documented. She said they brought back many happy memories. Her memory was amazing, and her mind as alert as ever.

The Queen Mum spent nearly an hour enjoying my photographs. I was thrilled when, before leaving the library, she signed my visitors' book. Her visit was a great honour and probably the highlight of my life as a Royalist.

Some weeks later, I spoke to The Queen about her mother's visit to my exhibition. I told her what an honour it had been, and she said, 'She told me how much she had enjoyed it.'

CLARENCE HOUSE
S.W.1

9th December, 1991

Dear Mr. Edwards,

I write to acknowledge your latest
letter to Queen Elizabeth The Queen Mother, and
the newspaper cutting you enclosed.

These have been read with interest, and
it is hoped that at least one of the many
photographs you have entered in a competition
wins a prize.

Yours sincerely,

Angela Oswald

Lady-in-Waiting

R. C. Edwards, Esq.,

The Queen Mother was the first member of the Royal Family to celebrate a 100th birthday (in 2000), and all her thousands of fans had looked forward to this historic occasion for some time. Arrangements were different from previous years. Instead of meeting and greeting her fans at Clarence House, she drove in an open flower-bedecked carriage with the Prince of Wales to Buckingham Palace. There, she appeared on the balcony with The Queen, Princess Margaret and the rest of the Royal Family. The cheering from the crowds in front of the railings was deafening.

I have the most happy and wonderful memories of her birthday celebrations.

Clarence House, London, 4th August 2001

HM The Queen Mother's 101st Birthday
4th August 2001

A few days before celebrating her 101st birthday, The Queen Mother was admitted to hospital. She was, however, determined not to disappoint her many fans who had gathered to give their warm wishes at Clarence House. She looked very frail – but in good spirits – as she greeted people from her buggy. When she stopped in front of me, I asked if I could read her birthday poem to her as I had done for many years previous. She said, 'Of course you can.'

I was just about to begin when a bodyguard stepped forward and snatched it out of my hand. The Queen Mum saw and demanded he give it back to me, saying, 'He always reads his poem to me.' Looking rather sheepish, the bodyguard handed it back, and I proceeded to read it aloud. Her Majesty looked very moved and thanked me, 'That was one of your best!'

At the age of 101 The Queen Mother was still indomitable and quite capable of making her own decisions. Sadly, she passed away eight months later whilst sleeping peacefully, her daughter holding her hand.

The Queen Mother and Dame Vera Lynn, St. Paul's Cathedral, London, May 1999
National treasures who became close friends during the Second World War

I had met Dame Vera two years before this photograph was taken, when we were both guests on Esther Rantzen's television show. The episode was a tribute to The Queen Mother on the sixtieth anniversary of her coronation as Queen Consort in May 1937.

After the programme ended I was delighted to be introduced to Dame Vera and her husband the late Harry Lewis. She kindly posed for a photograph and gave me her autograph. It was such an honour meeting a living legend.

Clarence House, London, 4th August 1992

On Thursday 28th March 2002 I travelled to Brittany with a group of friends to stay with French hosts in our twin town. Two days later, breaking news interrupted the television broadcast. I have a reasonable knowledge of French and had no difficulty translating: '*Elizabeth la reine mère de Grand-Bretagne est morte*' (Elizabeth, The Queen Mother of Great Britain is dead). I was speechless for several minutes and quite emotional.

Her death at the age of 101 cannot be described as unexpected as she had been in poor health and frail for several months. I'm sure that the death of Princess Margaret, at the age of seventy-one, just weeks earlier had deeply affected The Queen Mother. Amazingly, she was well enough to attend the funeral at Saint George's Chapel on 15th February – the fiftieth anniversary of the funeral of her father, King George VI.

We returned to the UK on 2nd April, and I immediately made arrangements to travel to London for our beloved Queen Mum's state funeral at Westminster a week later.

I arrived at the Abbey at midday on the 8th April with my sleeping bag and garden chair. Later that afternoon, I queued for nearly an hour for Her Majesty's lying-in-state in Westminster Hall. I can honestly say that seeing her coffin (on the catafalque covered with her personal standard, her crown and wreath of white flowers from The Queen) in the silence of the great hall was one of the most emotional experiences of my life.

The funeral procession the following morning was very impressive, with all the senior members of the Royal Family (with the exception of The Queen) walking solemnly behind the coffin. The sight of the Prince of Wales looking so bereft and mourning his beloved granny was heartbreaking.

After the service the coffin was taken to Saint George's Chapel for burial alongside the King in the private chapel.

The Queen Mother, during eight decades of public life, had endeared herself to generations of people with her warmth and friendliness. She was a national treasure and will never be forgotten.

The Queen Mother's funeral, London, 9th April 2002

CHAPTER 3
Diana, Princess of Wales 1961-1997

My interest in Diana started with her engagement to Prince Charles in February 1981. I travelled to London on 28th July and camped out at St Paul's Cathedral for the "wedding of the century" the following day. I met a young German man there (we are still good friends), and, on the evening before the wedding, we went to Hyde Park together and saw the magnificent firework display.

The atmosphere at St Paul's the next day was, of course, incredible, with people from all over the world attending. We had a superb view of the carriages arriving at the cathedral and joined in the service, which was relayed on loud speakers.

Although exhausted after a sleepless night, I managed to see Charles and Diana arriving at Waterloo Station to board their train en route to Broadlands in Hampshire to start their honeymoon.

During the next sixteen years I met Diana at many of her walkabouts and became a familiar face. She soon began to recognise me. When we met, I talked to her about her boys, her charities and her foreign visits; conversation was always very easy with Diana. She was warm, friendly and had a great sense of humour.

I was devastated when I heard about her tragic death on 31st August 1997 and immediately made arrangements to travel to London on 5th September for her funeral at Westminster Abbey the next day.

I camped out on The Mall with her admirers – not only Britons but people from many countries – and felt so pleased that I had been fortunate enough to have met Diana so many times. It was hard to accept that I would never see her again, but my photographs bring back so many happy memories.

I visited Althorp twice, and seeing the small island in the lake where she is buried was incredibly moving.

In 1998, the year after her death, I held exhibitions of my photographs of her in several towns and cities, including London, and was deeply moved by the reaction of visitors, many of whom became quite emotional.

Diana, "The People's Princess", will never be forgotten, and her sons, William and Harry, are her legacy.

May she rest in peace.

Diana was with Prince Andrew when I took this photograph. It was my first picture of her. They were on their way to Trooping the Colour, 1981.

This event will always be remembered. It was on this day that shots were fired at The Queen just as she arrived at Horse Guards Parade.

Above: Derby, February 1985

Below: Nottingham, March 1985

Chatsworth Park, Derbyshire, September 1987

Manchester, March 1993

By 1988 I had met Diana several times. It was in the April of that year that she greeted me personally. When I met her in Hanley, Staffordshire, she smiled at me and said, 'Hello, Colin, it's nice to see you again.'

I was so surprised that all I could say was, 'You know my name, Diana.' Rather cheekily, she replied, 'Yes, Colin, I know all about you!'

Charles and Diana took William and Harry – then aged six and four years old – to the Royal Tournament in 1988. As they approached me, she said to them, 'Boys, come and meet my friend, Colin' and they promptly shook hands with me.

Garter Day, Windsor, June 1986

Derby, February 1985

Above: Nottingham, January 1993

Below: Manchester, March 1991

I love this photograph of Diana. I met her as she arrived at The Midland Hotel, Manchester, in November 1988. I gave her early Christmas gifts, chocolates and sweets for William and Harry. She thanked me for them and said, 'The boys will love them.'

Manchester, January 1990   Manchester, January 1990

Diana returned to Manchester on my birthday in 1990. When I told her it was a special day, she wished me a happy birthday, and upon learning my age Diana's unexpected reply was, 'Oh, you're twenty years older than me!' She had such a wicked sense of humour.

Weston-Super-Mare, May 1986

Diana carried out two walkabouts in Manchester city centre in March 1991. I had taken the day off work so attended both. She must have noticed as on the second one she said, laughing, 'I think you're following me, Colin!'

Manchester, March 1991

London, June 1995

London, September 1995

Glossop, Derbyshire, June 1990

Leeds, May 1993

Above: Birmingham, March 1992

Below: Altrincham, July 1992

As they walked back to Sandringham House after the Christmas Day church service in 1993, Diana brought Harry over and said to him, 'Harry, this is Colin, he follows me everywhere.'

Above: Wrexham, July 1991

Opposite: Altrincham, July 1992

Below: Southport, June 1992

On the day after my birthday, Diana attended a charity lunch. On her walkabout later she wished me a happy birthday, and I gave her two photographs – one for William and one for Harry. She thanked me for them and said, 'The boys love your photos, Colin.' I was very touched. Diana had a way of making everyone feel special.

London, February 1994

I met Diana on her walkabout outside Great Ormond Street Hospital in February 1994 and gave her a Valentine's Day card.

I started to read the affectionate verse to her, and she interrupted, 'Colin, I'm freezing, if this was the Mediterranean, I'd talk to you all day!' A few days later, I received a thank you letter from her. She had a fantastic sense of humour.

Leeds, May 1993

This photograph was taken at my exhibition in Macclesfield library in April 1998. I was overwhelmed by the number of people who attended, which I think was testimony to Diana's popularity.

The photograph I am holding is one I took outside Liverpool Cathedral on a cold, dull day. A man standing next to me had made her laugh. This is one of my favourite images of Diana. We heard later that she had recorded her infamous *Panorama* interview two days previously. This photograph was selected by the *Daily Mail* for the cover of the magazine marking the first anniversary of her death on 31st August 1998.

In December 1996 I met Diana in London. As I waited, a young lady stood next to me. She told me she had flown in from Greece that morning to give flowers to Diana.

When Diana approached, the young lady was overcome and unable to speak. I told Diana about the lady's journey, and she said, 'That's incredible, I hope I've been worth it!' The young lady left on cloud nine.

Credit: Mark Stewart

London, January 1996

At 8am on Sunday 31st August 1997, I was woken up by someone knocking at my back door. I rushed downstairs, and standing in the rain was my neighbour. He knew how much I loved Diana and that I had met her on many occasions. He said to me, 'Sorry to wake you up, but I thought you should know... Diana is dead.'

It took me a few moments to process the shocking news. My neighbour explained that Diana and Dodi Fayed had been killed in a car crash in a tunnel in Paris. He told me to put the television on as all the channels were covering the tragedy.

I could hardly believe what I was hearing: this beautiful young lady, only thirty-six years of age, whom I had met so many times during the last sixteen years, had died in such tragic circumstances.

My phone rang all morning with calls from friends who were as upset as me. One of the calls came from a BBC researcher for the programme *Kilroy*, inviting me to take part in a tribute to Diana the following morning. I travelled down to London that evening and took the opportunity to pay my respects, as many others had, outside Kensington Palace. I was deeply affected by the number of tributes people were leaving at the gates, and the silence was overwhelming.

I returned to my hotel and continued to watch reports of Diana's death before trying to get some sleep.

The next morning, I was taken to the *Kilroy* studio. There, I met three friends who, like me, had met Diana many times over the years. I also recognised several famous people, friends of Diana, and reporters who had covered her engagements.

After lunch a friend and I took flowers to place amongst the thousands of tributes at the gates of Kensington Palace. I returned home that evening emotionally exhausted, but I knew I would have to return to London for the funeral.

On Friday 5th September I travelled back to the city with my sleeping bag and camped out on The Mall in anticipation of the funeral procession to Westminster the following morning. I was surrounded by people who loved Diana from all over the world, and strangers soon became friends; we were united in mourning "The People's Princess". My most poignant memory of that saddest of days is of HM The Queen's moving tribute and the heartbreaking sight of the young princes, William and Harry, walking slowly behind their beloved mother's coffin. I felt it was important to be in London for Diana's funeral, just as I had been for her wedding and the start of her public life sixteen years earlier.

Diana's funeral procession, London, 6th September 1997

CHAPTER 4

Weddings

The Royal Wedding of the Prince and Princess of Wales
29th July 1981

The wedding of Charles and Diana had been eagerly anticipated since their engagement was announced. I travelled to London the day before the ceremony with my sleeping bag and enough food and drink for the next twenty-four hours.

People had obviously been arriving all morning, but I soon found a place behind the barrier outside Saint Paul's Cathedral and was joined by a young man from Germany and many other people from all over the world.

That evening, my new friend and I went to Hyde Park to watch the firework display, which was accompanied by superb music; the atmosphere was amazing! We returned to Saint Paul's, and the pavement was covered with hundreds of sleeping bags and tents.

The crowds were singing all night, so sleeping was impossible. At 6am the police asked everyone to get up and fold away their tents. The weather was perfect – warm and sunny.

We had a fantastic view of the Royal carriages, and I'll never forget the roars of cheers as the Glass Coach arrived. Diana was accompanied by her father, Lord Spencer, and I could see she was holding his hand. She must have been overwhelmed by the cheering; it was deafening.

The service was relayed, and we all joined in, singing along with the hymns and cheering each time the couple made their vows. Afterwards, the new Prince and Princess of Wales returned to Buckingham Palace in the 1902 State Landau. I called out, 'Congratulations', and Diana wore a brilliant smile.

After exchanging addresses with my new German friend, I travelled to Waterloo station to see the couple depart on their journey to Broadlands, where they began their honeymoon. I slept for most of my own train journey as I headed home – I was exhausted after a sleepless night and the excitement of an historic day.

BUCKINGHAM PALACE

20th November, 1981

Dear Mr. Edwards,

    The Prince and Princess of Wales have asked
me to write and thank you for your very kind
thought in writing to them on the occasion of
their marriage.

    Their Royal Highnesses were most touched by
the good wishes you have expressed and have asked
me to send you their very sincere thanks.

Yours sincerely,

Jim Kirby

The Wedding of the Duke and Duchess of York
23rd July 1986

The Queen and Prince Philip's second son, Prince Andrew, married Sarah Ferguson at Westminster Abbey four months after announcing their engagement. Sarah had become very popular. People warmed to her friendly personality.

I travelled, once again, by coach overnight and arrived in London in the early hours to secure a position between Admiralty Arch and the top of Whitehall. The weather was warm, dry and sunny, just as it had been for Charles and Diana's wedding five years earlier. Only Great Britain could stage a spectacular event with such pomp and pageantry that people from miles away flocked to experience it. On their return to the Palace after the ceremony, the new Duke and Duchess of York looked so happy. I remember Sarah held her large bouquet high in the air for the crowds to see.

Once all the carriages had passed, I made my way down The Mall with thousands of people to see the newly married couple and the Royal Family on the palace balcony. Although I was quite a long way from the railings, the atmosphere was fantastic, and I could just about see the kiss. Later, I saw Andrew and Sarah in their carriage on their way to Victoria Station to start their honeymoon. They were accompanied by a massive teddy bear!

During the next ten years – until their divorce in 1996 – I met Sarah several times, and, like Diana, she was always warm and friendly, often greeting me personally.

In 1988 their first daughter was born, and they have been wonderful parents to Princess Beatrice and Princess Eugenie.

The Wedding of the Earl and Countess of Wessex
19th June 1999

The Queen's youngest son, Prince Edward, married Sophie Rhys Jones at St George's Chapel, Windsor Castle, on 19th June 1999. Their wedding was low-key compared with the weddings of Edward's siblings, with no pageantry or balcony appearance. However, hundreds of well-wishers arrived in Windsor early on the morning of the wedding. My friend and I had been successful in the ballot for tickets to stand near the chapel. We had an excellent view of the Royal Family and guests arriving, and there were huge cheers for Edward and his brothers, Charles and Andrew, as they walked from the castle to the chapel. But the loudest cheers were reserved for The Queen and Prince Philip, and for Sophie and her father. After the service the Earl and Countess of Wessex drove through the town in an open carriage.

The Queen, who has a warm and close relationship with her daughter-in-law, must feel so happy that Edward's marriage has been such a success.

They have two children: Lady Louise Windsor, who was a bridesmaid at William and Kate's wedding in 2011, and James, Viscount Severn.

I have had the pleasure of meeting Sophie several times, and she is always warm, friendly and down-to-earth.

The Wedding of the Duke and Duchess of Cambridge 29th April 2011

The engagement of Prince William and Kate Middleton was announced in November 2010, and excitement accelerated over the following five months until the wedding at Westminster Abbey on 29th April 2011.

I think I was probably one of the first members of the public to meet Kate after she became a royal figure. She and William carried out their first official engagement together on 24th February 2011 at Trearddur Bay, Anglesey, when they launched a new lifeboat. Their home was only a few miles away, near RAF valley, where William was a search and rescue helicopter pilot.

My friends and I waited for four hours in the bitter cold to see William and Kate arrive at the lifeboat station. Following the ceremony and a short service, they crossed the road to start their walkabouts. Kate looked so beautiful and confident as she accepted my friend's posy. She graciously allowed me to kiss her hand, which brought back poignant memories for me of her fiancé's late mother. I gave Kate two photographs – one of Diana and one of William and Harry with their mother. I told her how much I was looking forward to the wedding and that I intended on camping out on The Mall. She said, 'I hope it doesn't rain!' Fortunately, it didn't.

The night before the wedding was dry but very cold. By midnight we were surrounded by hundreds of people in sleeping bags and tents who had gathered from all over the world. I found it hard to believe that almost thirty years had passed since I had experienced the same atmosphere at William's parent's wedding day on 29th July 1981. How proud Diana would have been of her son and daughter-in-law.

We had an excellent view of Kate and her father, and the Royal Family as they made their way to the Abbey. We were also in a good position to see William and Kate, The Duke and Duchess of Cambridge, returning to the palace in the open 1902 State Landau (also used by Charles and Diana, and Andrew and Sarah). Due to the vast number of people, it was impossible to get to the front of the palace for the balcony appearance and the two kisses!

I returned home just in time for the highlights on television. I had thoroughly enjoyed my fourth Royal wedding – perhaps the fifth one will be Harry's in the not so distant future...

Prince Harry, best man, with his cousin, Lady Louise Windsor, bridesmaid, and Tom Pettifer, page boy.

CHAPTER 5
Other Members of the Royal Family

In addition to Her Majesty The Queen, The Queen Mother and Diana, Princess of Wales, I have had the privilege of meeting many members of the Royal Family.

Buckingham Palace, April 1986

Clarence House, London, 4th August 1994

Trooping the Colour, London, June 2011 (Kate's first appearance at the ceremony)

Sarah, Duchess of York. Manchester, April 1997

I first met the late Princess Margaret in 1989 during a visit to Manchester. She was very petite and had the most beautiful complexion and deep blue eyes. She was always very friendly, and whenever I was fortunate enough to meet her, she always recognised me and would greet me personally.

Manchester, July 1996

Crewe, October 1996

HRH Princess Margaret

Above: Birmingham, June 1995

Below: Wolferton, Norfolk, August 1996

HRH Princess Alexandra. London, June 1997

Sophie, Countess of Wessex. Staffordshire, September 2011

HRH The Duchess of Cornwall. St Asaph, July 2012

HRH The Prince of Wales

From the mid 1960s through until 1981, I had only ever seen Prince Charles at Royal events. It was not until November 1981 that I spoke to him for the first time. I met him outside the Royal Albert Hall as he and Diana left after the Festival of Remembrance. I shook his hand, and he thanked me for the photographs I gave him of their wedding day. As they drove away, I just caught a glimpse of him showing Diana the photographs.

Since then I have many poignant memories of meeting the Prince. I met him outside the Free Trade Hall in Manchester in December 1983, after he and Diana had attended a charity carol concert, but it was in May 1984 that they both recognised me as I waited amongst the crowd during a walkabout in Chester.

In March 1997 I was filmed meeting him in Wolverhampton as part of a BBC documentary I was involved with. On that occasion I gave him a photograph of The Queen Mother to which he said, 'Another great photo of my grandmother.' Later that year, I of course saw him from a distance on The Mall during the funeral of Diana, and I offered my condolences when I met him a few weeks later in Manchester.

More recently, I have met him with Camilla, whom he married in April 2005. I have always admired Charles' interests in architecture, the arts and the environment, but I think his greatest achievement has been The Prince's Trust, which has helped thousands of young people.

Above: Conwy, July 2002

Below: Edinburgh, July 1994

HRH The Prince of Wales and HRH The Duchess of Cornwall

Charles and Camilla, St Asaph
9th July 2012

Charles, Prince of Wales and Camilla, Duchess of Cornwall visited St Asaph Cathedral in Denbighshire during their tour of North Wales on 9th July 2012. The purpose of their visit was to celebrate the town receiving city status, as granted by HM The Queen during her Diamond Jubilee year. St Asaph is now one of the smallest cities in the country.

Following their visit to the cathedral, Charles and Camilla carried out a walkabout, where they met many local people. This was the first time I met The Duchess of Cornwall.

As Charles approached me, he said, 'I haven't seen you for some time.' I shook his hand and said how pleased I was to be seeing him on that occasion. I gave him a photograph of himself and William in the Garter procession at Windsor, just before Camilla joined us. She asked me if we had met before, and I replied, 'No, we haven't, but I'm so pleased to meet you today.' She kindly posed for a photograph, and I gave her a card for her upcoming birthday. I was so surprised to receive a personal thank you note from her a few weeks later. Camilla was warm, friendly and down-to-earth. I was pleased to have met her.

St Asaph, July 2012

Garter Day, Windsor, June 1996
HRH The Princess Royal and
HRH The Prince of Wales

Garter Day, Windsor, June 2008
HRH Prince William and
HRH The Prince of Wales

On this occasion William's grandmother, HM The Queen, installed him as the 1000th knight of the Garter. Diana would have been so proud.

HRH Prince William. Lancashire, April 2011

HRH Prince William, London, June 2002   HRH Prince Harry, Sandringham, December 1997

TRH Princes William and Harry

On the 4th August 1982 I travelled to London for the christening of Prince William. It was a lovely day, and I stood by Buckingham Palace to see Charles, Diana and the baby prince arrive in their car. Everyone in the crowd was thrilled when Diana held him up so we could all catch a glimpse.

I first met William and Harry in 1988 when Diana spotted me in the crowd at the Royal Tournament and introduced me to the young princes as her friend, Colin. I shook each of their hands and told them how pleased I was to meet them.

More recently, I met William with his fiancée in Anglesey, and I of course watched their 2011 wedding with great delight.

Catherine, Duchess of Cambridge. Anglesey, February 2011

Nottingham, June 2012

Birth of HRH Prince George of Cambridge

The first child of TRH The Duke and Duchess of Cambridge was born on 22nd July 2013 at St Mary's hospital in London, where both William and Harry were born. The baby prince is third in line to the throne.

William and Kate's son makes royal history by becoming the third living heir. This has not happened in the British Monarchy since Queen Victoria was on the throne. HM The Queen's long reign has meant that Prince Charles is now the longest serving heir apparent in history, with sixty-one years as her immediate successor. The previous record of fifty-nine years was set by his great-great grandfather Edward VII.

The baby prince is The Queen's third great-grandchild and the first grandchild for The Prince of Wales. I am sure William and Kate will be excellent parents, and I look forward to meeting Prince George in the future.

The Future for the Royal Family and Me

Since the spectacular and unforgettable Diamond Jubilee celebrations in 2012, the Royal Family is more popular than it has been for many years.

There will be much to celebrate during the next decade. In September 2015 The Queen will break the record of Queen Victoria and will have reigned longer than any King or Queen in the history of the monarchy. The following year, on 21st April 2016, Her Majesty will celebrate her ninetieth birthday – the first monarch to become a nonagenarian!

There is much to look forward to. If the Queen continues to enjoy good health, she will celebrate her Platinum Jubilee in 2022 and her 100th birthday in 2026, as her beloved mother did in 2000, and she will have reigned for an incredible seventy-four years! The celebrations will be amazing.

On the Queen's death Charles will succeed his mother as King Charles III. Even though his reign will be short, I do believe he will be a popular and successful monarch.

In the years to come I think that the reign of King William V and Queen Catherine will be every bit as successful and popular as the long reign of his grandmother HM Queen Elizabeth II.

William and Kate have already shown, since their wedding in 2011, how easily they relate to ordinary people. They are both warm, kind and caring, and by the time William succeeds to the throne, they will have a young family to support them. Harry too, either single or married, will be a tremendous support for his brother. It will be an incredibly popular Royal Family!

Sadly, I will not be around to cheer William and Kate at their coronation, but I intend to meet and photograph Her Majesty and other members of her family as often as possible over the next few years.

The Queen's Coronation sixty years ago was the start of my amazing and eventful life.

Acknowledgements

I would like to thank Her Majesty The Queen for the many kindnesses shown to me during the last thirty years. I am also most grateful to the the Buckingham Palace Information Officers and the staff of the Lieutenancy Offices throughout the country for information about the engagements of the Royal Family.

Finally, I would like to thank Shaun Russell of Candy Jar Books for agreeing to publish this book and for all his help and advice.

Additional Captions